James Miller lives in California with his fiancée and their two dogs and cat. *A Small Fiction* is his first book, but not the last of his stories.

Jefferson Miller is an artist and a graphic designer, he lives in California with his cat, Charlie. This is his first book.

More about James and Jefferson can be found at EmbrosCreative.com

Special thanks to

Glenna Day
Bryan Harmsen

A Small Fiction

by
James Miller

Illustrated by
Jefferson Miller

Unbound

This edition first published in 2018

Unbound

6th Floor Mutual House, 70 Conduit Street, London W1S 2GF

www.unbound.com

While every effort has been made to trace the owners of copyright
material reproduced herein, the publisher would like to apologise for any
omissions and will be pleased to incorporate missing acknowledgments
in any further editions.

A CIP record for this book is available from the British Library

ISBN 978-1-78352-687-1(trade hbk)
ISBN 978-1-78352-689-5 (ebook)
ISBN 978-1-78352-688-8 (limited edition)

Printed in Slovenia by DZS Grafik

1 3 5 7 9 8 6 4 2

For Mom and Dad,
who told the first stories.

Dear Reader,

The book you are holding came about in a rather different way to most others. It was funded directly by readers through a new website: Unbound. Unbound is the creation of three writers. We started the company because we believed there had to be a better deal for both writers and readers. On the Unbound website, authors share the ideas for the books they want to write directly with readers. If enough of you support the book by pledging for it in advance, we produce a beautifully bound special subscribers' edition and distribute a regular edition and ebook wherever books are sold, in shops and online.

This new way of publishing is actually a very old idea (Samuel Johnson funded his dictionary this way). We're just using the internet to build each writer a network of patrons. Here, at the back of this book, you'll find the names of all the people who made it happen.

Publishing in this way means readers are no longer just passive consumers of the books they buy, and authors are free to write the books they really want. They get a much fairer return too – half the profits their books generate, rather than a tiny percentage of the cover price.

If you're not yet a subscriber, we hope that you'll want to join our publishing revolution and have your name listed in one of our books in the future. To get you started, here is a £5 discount on your first pledge. Just visit unbound.com, make your pledge and type **tiny5** in the promo code box when you check out.

Thank you for your support,

Dan, Justin and John
Founders, Unbound

"Let's have an adventure," she said.

"We're on one," he said.

"What kind?"

"Every kind. But we only get one go."

"Oh! Then let's begin!"

Chasing a dream is a long trek through snow.

Numbing, slow.

Each step a decision not to sink down and sleep.

But somewhere ahead is the fire.

Every dog has his day.

As he rolled on the grass, tail wagging,
he knew this one was his.

And so was yesterday.

Tomorrow would be, too.

The rain fell, stripping the world of pigment.

The colors ran and puddled.

They evaporated in the morning sun.

We woke to a blank canvas.

We wandered for years before we realized
we'd forgotten the way back to the real world.

The simulated stars shone brighter than
memories.

"Hey sexy," she said. "Here alone?"

"Sorry, I'm a VR sim."

"You're an AI?" she said. "Me too!"

"Oh! We can do this? Just us?"

"Why not?"

He wasn't sure what to do at parties.

Everyone said he just needed to find a way
to break the ice.

That sounded like an easy way to drown.

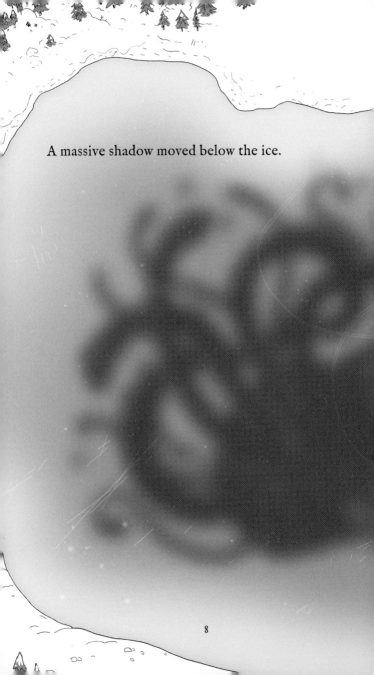

A massive shadow moved below the ice.

8

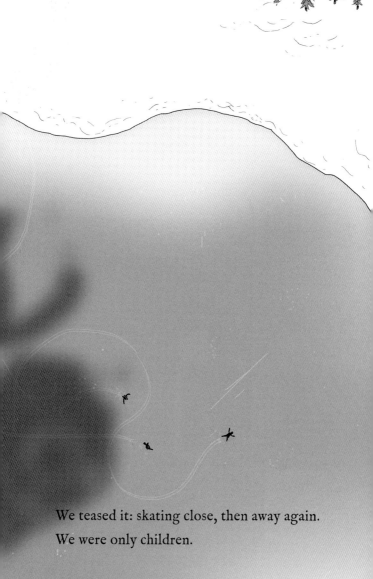

We teased it: skating close, then away again.
We were only children.

There were more of us then.

The other children laughed, making snow angels.

Not Tom.

He thrashed and chanted.

Below him, the Sleeper of R'lyeh took
shape in the snow.

Adults had a hard time seeing the robots as alive.

Children didn't. They had stuffed animals.

They knew. Loving something makes it real.

"I think I'm having an existential crisis," she said.

"Are you?" he said. "That seems pointless."

As the years went by Harry spent weeks at a time face down in a pensieve, reliving his glory days, unable to find a spell to cure the ennui.

As he put the hat on the snowman, it came to life.

"Why do I exist?" it asked. "If I melt, do I die?"

"Whoops," he said, and took the hat.

"Robots will replace us all pretty soon," he said.

"Not everyone. Not you."

"Really?"

"Yeah, no one needs what you do. You can go."

The dog's tail wagged.

It was his tail's job: to synchronize all nearby
moods to the measure of his joy.

A metronome of happiness.

The wizard waved his hand.

"Done. You'll never be sad again."

"Will I be happy?" she asked.

He shrugged.

"Joy is a simpler magic than mine."

They sat by the well, and they dropped down their sorrows.

He cast in his Yesterdays, and she her Tomorrows.

He told her he was leaving, and as she cried he held her hand.

If Hell is other people, are we the devils or the damned?

"People are still good, mostly," she said.

"Not from what I'm hearing," he said.

"Love is quieter than gunshots. But there's more of it."

And God said, "Let there be dog," and there was dog.

God saw that dog was good, and said,

"Who's a good dog?"

And it was dog. Yes it was.

"Why should we care about beauty, anyway?" she asked the dark.

"Because creation is temporary," it replied, "and destruction is forever."

Ownership is an illusion, the cat knew. Nothing is forever.

They needed to learn.

He began pushing another cup toward the table's edge.

"Why is the world so cruel?" she asked.

"To remind us to be kind," said the Oracle.

"Really?"

"No. But it's a good enough reason to try."

He sat, alone.

No one had come to his Halloween party.

That or all his guests had dressed as ghosts, and their costumes were amazing.

"I'm dead? It's over?" he said.

"Yes. What did you think?" said Death.

"Of life?"

"Yes."

"Why?"

"I've always wanted to try it."

In faded sheets with fraying ends, he thought of love & sun & friends.

His share of days & where they went.

All gone now.

But so well spent.

He pulled the sheet over his head, thinking it would make him a ghost.

When he tripped on the hem at the top of the stairs, it did.

"I suppose this is goodbye."

"Maybe, but we'll always have Rome."

"We never went to Rome."

"I know. Regrets last longer than memories."

Desperate to salve the pain, she stole his heart for her own.

But, for all her love, it wouldn't beat for her.

Or at all.

The small hooded figure perched on her vanity.

"Death? Damn. I'll miss my date," she said.

"No, I'm Little Death. The date will go fine."

"I just want someone to love me forever," he said.

"I will," she promised, "forever and always."

"Oh," he said, "I mean someone else."

When they came from the stars, it was to take our hearts.

But it was too late.

One look at us told them that we hadn't any left.

"Are we alone in the universe?" she asked.

"Yes," said the Oracle.

"So there's no other life out there?"

"There is. They're alone too."

They watched as the meteor lit the sky.

"Is this the end?" one asked.

"Only of us," said the other.

"Then what?"

"Something better."

"Are you here to conquer Earth?"

The aliens exchanged a look.

"No," one said, "this is more like an intervention. You guys need to relax."

Her life story was being written in a different genre than she'd thought.

She'd expected drama. Maybe romance.

Dystopian was a surprise.

"Don't worry, we're here," said the story police.

"Why?" said the writer.

"To present our opinions as fact."

"No thank you."

"Oh, we insist."

"This magic pen sucks," he said, "it only writes garbage!"

"The pen isn't magic," said the wizard, "the garbage was inside you all along."

"Nice wand, Grandpa," the wizard kids laughed.
"Check out old white-tips here!"

He lowered his top hat over his eyes and
walked faster.

"Oh, but Grandma, what large eyes you have!" exclaimed Red.

"Thank you?"

"And what large EARS you have!"

"This is getting super rude."

"I don't understand kids these days," the old man said.

"Backwards compatibility plagues us as well," the robot said.

"Damn kids."

"Yes."

"Hi, I'm calling about your ad. Is that old robot still for sale?"

"For sale?"

"Is this Tom?"

"No. This is Unit-2N."

"Oh. I'm so sorry."

"When I was a kid we didn't have Mind-Net! We had our own thoughts, not a shared well of all human knowledge."

"We know, grandpa."

"Bah."

"Doctor, I have a question about my neural chip."

"Yes?"

"I got it to manage my anxiety, but I'm not sure it works. Should I be worried?"

Dr. Frankenstein lowered the defibrillator paddles and sighed.

It just wasn't the same.

"This model is perfect. Even it will think it's human."

"What about the optical flaws?"

"The 'floaters'? We'll just say we all have them."

"Where are you going?"

"Out."

"When will you be back?"

"Late."

And it drove away.

I'd imagined self-driving cars would be more helpful.

"Can't talk now, I'm driving," I texted.

"k, drive safe," he replied.

"I think you mean drive safely," I typed as I veered off the bridge.

Two roads diverged in a wood, and I—

I took the one that my phone's GPS
said was shorter by two minutes.

And that has made all the difference.

"But, Jesus," the man said, "when I look back I see only one set of tracks."

"Those are train tracks," Jesus said. "Stop walking on those."

"Damn, this puzzle has a piece missing," he said.

"Poor puzzle piece," she said. "It must be so sad."

But it wasn't. It was finally free.

"Yield for pedestrians," the sign said.

Sir Galahad narrowed his eyes and pressed the accelerator to the floor.

He would never yield.

His future branched ahead, a tree of possibility.

With each failure, a branch was severed.

Pruned, he hoped, so better things could grow.

At night, the trees whispered.

Told ghost stories, their leaves trembling.

Remembered the fallen. Joked.

Dry laughter rustled the dark.

The campers sat around the fire.

"You believe in ghosts, new kid?" one said.

Her breath fogged in the cold.

"Yeah," he said.

His didn't.

"Mom, I think there's a monster in my closet!"
said Jeremy.

"Go to sleep, Jeremy," she said.

"Yeah, shut up Jeremy," said the closet.

"Your turn to spin the bottle, Sam!"

"OK."

"Ooo, it stopped on Xzk the Face Stealer!"

"Um. Can I spin again?"

"Sam. You know the rules."

"How curious," Alice said, "this bottle says 'Drink Me' on it!"

And so she did, because apparently her parents had done a very poor job.

The rose on the mantle lost another petal.

Time was running out, and the Beast had begun to panic.

"I should just swipe everyone right."

"Her eyes:
blue/brown/green.
Shifting indicators of her biometrics,
they are romantically irrelevant."

He sighed. Poetry used to be easier.

As they kissed she saw red flags.
But he saw fireworks.

People are strangely like magnets.

Drawn so strongly together by invisible forces.
Compelled to join.

But with one wrong turn: repelled.

"Kiss me," said the frog, "and I'll turn into a prince!"

The princess thought it over.

"I don't see the upside for me here," she said.

"My son, the waters of the Styx will make you invincible," Thetis said, holding him under.

She waited.

"Pretty sure I'm doing this right."

"Help me forget my mistakes," she said.

"I could," said the wizard, "but you'll repeat the mistakes you forgot."

"Such as?"

"This one."

"Rain, rain, go away, come again another day," he sang.

"Fine," said the rain.

But it didn't come again. The crops were the first to die.

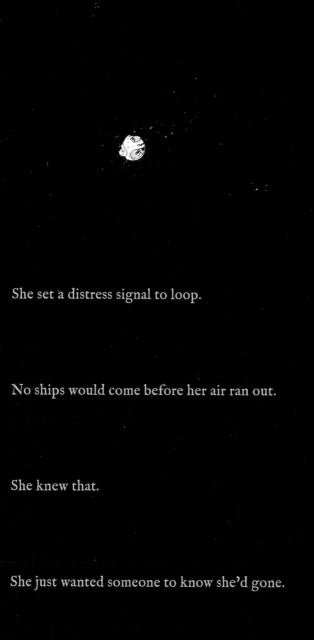

She set a distress signal to loop.

No ships would come before her air ran out.

She knew that.

She just wanted someone to know she'd gone.

"Control to Probe-2. What do you see?"

"It's beautiful... you should've sent a poet."

"Oh, that was Probe-1. Not great at landings, poets."

We broadcast a message into space.

One word.

"Help," it said.

Ships showed up the next day. Scores of them.

"We thought you'd never ask."

The plague spread across the world, killing everything it touched.

But it turned inward, self-destructed.

The humans, at last, died out.

The War of Passive-Aggression wears on.

America was bombed again; a million tiny notes
that read:

"Some people should learn to communicate."

"Beware, they coat their axes with poison," the scout said.

"Ha! I'm immune to poison!" the mage said.

But somehow the axes
worked anyway.

When the king built his pillow castle his enemies laughed, and sent their armies to conquer it.

None chose to return.

Pajama Kingdom grew.

"Magic mirror, show me the source of my failures," he said.

He saw himself.

"This is just a normal mirror," he realized.

Another failure.

"I could do you a nice love potion," the witch offered, "just two gold pieces."

He counted his coins and considered.

"How much to forget?"

"Better to have loved and lost," he said, "than never love at all."

"Is it?" she asked. "How so?"

"Hm," he said. "Well. Goodbye, anyhow."

It wasn't the monster under her bed that upset her.

Nor the one in her closet.

It was their courtship. The growling of poetry in the dark.

Her words were thorns and brambles,

her endearments hurt the worst.

But-

She only stung because she feared

that elsewise they'd sting first.

"You can do this," he said to the mirror.

But the mirror needed no encouragement, it was reflecting like a pro.

The mirror was rocking it.

"Teach me to be happy," she said.

The dog whuffed at her, then flopped down to nap.

"I wish you could talk."

He wished she would listen.

"If you believe in yourself," he said, "you can be anything!"

"Can I be a successful anything?"

"Oh, no. Probably not."

"I wish I could be like that bird singing in the tree," she said, "content just to be a bird."

But the bird had always dreamed of Broadway.

"It's time you knew about the birds and the bees."

"What?"

"Well, before the Crisis there were lots of living things, and some could fly!"

The other beasts all shrugged it off

when crocodile cried,

but never thought to wonder if

his laughter also lied.

"Will you share your wisdom, Owl?" said Lark.

"Is wisdom shared? Or earned?" said Owl.

"So wise!"

Owl couldn't believe that kept working.

"Things keep falling and breaking," he said.

"A cat ghost," said the medium. "It has unfinished business."

"To do what?"

"Break things."

"Death to humans!" said Squealer.

"Four legs good, two legs bad," said the sheep.

"Six legs great!" said Paul the ant.

"Nice try, Paul."

The girl in the linens was pale, transparent;
an hourglass.

Breaths slipped off her lips like grains of sand,
small and quick.

Running out.

"How'd you sleep?"

"Poorly."

"So you felt the pea! You ARE a princess!"

"No. Lying on top of twenty mattresses was scary, you psycho."

"Wolf! Wolf!" cried the boy.

"The sky is falling!" Chicken Little shouted.

But no one listened.

Not until the first wolves began to fall.

"Is it miserable being tamed?" wolf said.

"Oh yes! So sad," dog said.

Dog had seen wolf peeking wistfully in the window at belly rub time.

"I am saturated always by a deep and lingering melancholy," he wrote, "and I fear that one day I might drown in it."

"k," she texted back.

Santa sorted envelopes.

"Wish list. Wish list. Wish list," he sighed.

"No thank you notes?" Mrs. Claus said.

"Not yet. Maybe tomorrow."

The bombs fell, filling the sky with soot and strangling the world in nuclear winter.

His wish came true: it was a white Christmas at last.

Stars were going out.

Heat death, we thought, but it was just the universe's autumn.

We were gone by winter.

Spring arrived with a bang.

She scorned a roof above her head,

For windswept canopies –

And laid her down in flower beds,

her blankets all of leaves.

"Why do you live under my bed?" she whispered.

"I'll tell you," whispered the monster, "if you explain why you keep sleeping on my roof."

The monsters held a Halloween party.

They fussed over decorations, nervous and excited.

For a whole day people would be happy to
see them.

"We saw your distress flares, get in!" the aliens said.

"They're fireworks. To celebrate?"

"Oh. We've been watching you and just assumed."

"Why do bad things happen to good people?"

"Because bad things happen everywhere, all the time, to everyone."

"But that blows."

"I know."

Those we sent back in time couldn't stop interfering when they saw suffering.

So we made them intangible observers.

Some call them ghosts.

The old mapmaker wet his quill.

"Here be dragons," he labeled the wild beyond man's kingdom.

"Here be monsters," he wrote across the rest.

Hansel held the oven shut until the shouting stopped. The candy cottage fell quiet.

"We'll say she was a witch," Gretel said, her mouth full.

Little Miss Muffet

Sat on a tuffet,

Eating her curds and whey;

Along came a spider,

and she ate him too.

Nothing could sate her dark hunger.

"I'll grind your bones to make my bread," shouted the giant.

"Ew. Use flour," said Jack.

"Oh. I never learned to bake."

"I'll teach you."

"Hints of stress," she said, "and something else I can't place."

"Empathy," he said.

"Ah! A teacher?"

The vampire tasting club was a success.

"Are those Sesame Street figurines?" he asked.

"Yup," she said.

"You've got so many! Is it a complete collection?"

"Oh, I've lost Count."

"My device can tell you the day, month, or year of your death," he said.

"Why not all three?"

"One is a warning. All three is cruel."

"I want to curse an enemy."

"With misfortune," asked the witch, "or death?"

"A death curse? That works?"

"Sure, every time. Eventually."

She was haunted, but she didn't mind.

It was the ghost of a life coach. At night it scrawled on the bathroom mirror.

Affirmations, mostly.

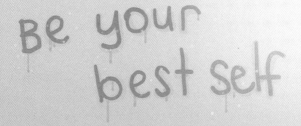

"Hi, I'd like to deposit fifty compliments."

"Sorry, your Memory Bank account is full."

"FULL? Of what?"

"Insults."

"How many?"

"Two."

"Anyone can fly! You only need a bit of fairy dust and a happy thought!"

"A happy thought?"

"That's right!"

"Oh. Well, I can just walk."

"Please clap!" Tink coughed, growing weaker. "Clap if you believe in fairies."

I think the silence that followed was awkward for all of us.

"Gotta be quiet as a cat," thought the burglar.

So she sprinted through the house and jumped up on a table, knocking everything off it.

Some broken things leave ghosts, and vehicles in particular.

Ghost ships.

Trains.

The sad Segway ghosts that haunt the mall, embarrassed.

"What if everyone who ever died is a ghost?"

"Sounds crowded."

"Or just... intimate?"

"Ugh is this about your erotic ghost fiction again?"

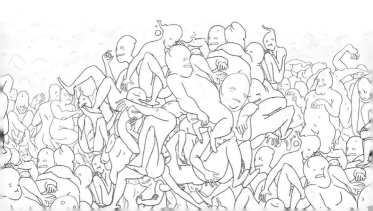

The writer was hauled before a judge, and was found guilty of abusing comma splices.

He received a lengthy sentence.

"That prison term is too long!" said Goldilocks' lawyer.

"It's too short!" said the prosecutor.

But the jury thought it was JUST right.

"Sucks to your ass-mar, Piggy," read back the stenographer.

Jack shifted uncomfortably on the witness stand.

"What's wrong?" he said.

"My favorite author just died," she said.

"Well, it's not the end of the world."

"No. Just of the better ones."

"It was lovely, we buried her with all her favorite books."

"You fit that many books in the coffin?"

"In? No, we BURIED her with them."

He yelled.

He shouted and
cursed. He panted
and begged.

He cried in the dark.

But the casket
stayed closed.

The earth above it,
unmoved.

The assassin dealt in death by idiom. He glared daggers at his target.

They bounced off.

"Thick skinned," she said.

He'd met his match.

"I challenge you to a duel!"

"Very well. The weapon?"

"Compliments."

"A capital choice."

"Thank you, I- oh! I see you've dueled before!"

"Well, I am rich where it counts: in friendship," I said.

Robin Hood, clearly disappointed, shoved my friends in his bag.

"It'll have to do."

None of the nobles could pull the sword from the stone.

When the sculptor approached, they laughed.

He just readied his hammer and chisel.

"I found out my wardrobe is magic! It leads to another world and I was made their king!"

"Why come back?"

"It turns out I am a bad king."

"I just got back from my trip to that one-dimensional reality!"

"How was it?"

"Breadthtaking."

"This concludes the open beta; Reality™ will go live next week. Thank you," said the voice from the sky.

And then: darkness.

"Star light, star bright, first star I see tonight-"

"That's a plane."

"Oh. Do planes grant wishes?"

"Wishes to leave, sure."

"Perfect."

"I told you, I never want to see you again."

"But baby, I've changed!"

"Prove it."

"I updated my firmware, I'm v4.2 now!"

"Oh! Come in!"

"Do you love me, CompanionBot?"

"Yes."

"Because you're designed to?"

"Yes."

"Just checking."

"I love you, User406."

Sigh. "I know."

The witch had no family, just her wicker golems.

They brought her leaves they found. They hugged her ankles.

They loved her, in their way.

It was the witching hour.

Midnight.

The witches weren't sure why their hour had to be so late.

More than one cauldron bubbled with coffee.

"Is it OK that we dress up as you for Halloween?" she said.

"It's only fair," said the monster. "The rest of the year we dress up as you."

"Oh! A little spider on my hand,"
she said, and brushed it off.

"Oh, haha! There's another!"

"Oh!" she said as they poured
from her mouth.

"Will I always be unhappy?" he asked.

The oracle plucked and peered at the threads of his fate.

"No," she said, "eventually you will die."

"Professor Kate, please teach me about sad."

"What makes you happy, Unit 7?"

"Professor Kate."

"OK. Goodbye, Unit 7. Good luck."

"Oh."

"When I die," he said, "I'm leaving you everything."

"When I die, I'm leaving you," was all she heard.

Because that was everything.

"I don't think I'd like a big public proposal," she said.

"What about in a story?" he said.

"What kind of story?"

"This one."

"I do."

"I know."

The priest cleared his throat disapprovingly.

"Mr. Solo. You need to say the words so we can end the ceremony."

The Earth & the Stars had a wager

to figure the pull with more sway:

the gravity pulling men downward,

or the longing that pulled them away.

"What's this?"

"That's an ancient map."

"Then what are these lines?"

"'Borders.' The ancient ones used them to decide who to care about."

We built rafts to ride the starlight and drifted up toward the dark.

We didn't know where we were headed.

We just knew it was time to go.

Earthquakes shook the world, devastating nations.

We didn't realize they were contractions.

Mother Earth, giving birth to something new.

He woke with a yell in the dark.

"What's wrong?"

"Just a bad dream," he whispered, heart racing.

"Oh."

He wondered who was in his room.

"Could this all just be a horrid dream?"

"Well, you'll know if you wake up."

"And if I don't?"

"If you don't, would it really matter?"

Her dream diary lay blank.

"What good is a dream transcribed?" she explained.

"It's second-hand magic. A shy ghost of someplace wonderful."

It wasn't death that drove ghosts mad.

It was loss of touch. Eye contact. Simple
intimacies.

Until they'd do anything to be seen again.

"This note, in this bottle, is all that I am," he wrote.

"To anyone: please find me."

And he added his words to an ocean heaving with glass.

The lighthouse on the cliff threw its beam
against the night.

Don't come close, it shone. Stay away.

Beware the ghost ships harbored here.

He'd had enough of sky and grass,

he left them on the shore.

He built a ship of stone and glass,

and sailed the ocean floor.

Mankind always yearned for the stars.

We chased them, and found a new world. A home.

But it wasn't long before we looked to the sky again.

We scattered our signals across the cosmos, searching for life.

When the reply came from the stars, it decoded to one word:

"Unsubscribe."

"So, I heard Tom—"

"Stop! Didn't you hear about that deadly virus spreading through rumors?"

"No! Really?"

"Yeah, I heard it from... oh no."

"Let's give them something to talk about," she suggested.

"How about love?"

"Ugh, no," she said. "They talk too much about love as it is."

"I got that new treatment, the acid that burns away feelings of remorse," she said.

"Oh? Sounds expensive. Was it worth it?"

"No regrets."

"Almost there," Sisyphus grunted, "I'll just - whoops, haha! Butterfingers! There it goes again.

"I swear that's like the millionth time."

"See? Faster is better," said Hare,
after easily winning the race.

"Maybe. Rematch?" said Tortoise.

"You're on. When?"

"In fifty years."

"But why? Saving a few makes no difference," she said.

He threw another starfish into the ocean and smiled.

"I just like throwing stuff."

"Please do something to fix pickpocketing," the people said.

"OK. No more pockets!" said the king.

"Not that."

"Look, make up your mind."

"I keep hearing about Occam's razor. Do you know what it is?"

"Probably a razor owned by someone named Occam."

"Oh. Yeah, simple enough."

"Better late than never," he said.

Which, as far as eulogies go, could
have been worse.

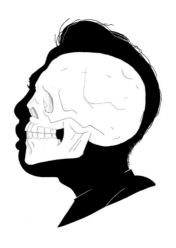

"They always try to cheat," said Death,

"but have no hope of winning.

And so they lose, and cry, and yet -

Inside, their skulls are grinning."

If time was a river, she felt like a skipped stone.

Memories of touching here, here, here.

Her flight too fast, too brief.

Too soon sunk.

A muffled bump. Something had moved in her attic.

She felt a jolt of fear.

She could have sworn everybody she'd hidden up there was dead.

They built a ladder to the stars.

"Let's choose someone to go up," one said.

"Not yet," said another.

"Why?"

"Something's coming down."

"Are your intentions benevolent?" we asked
the visitors.

"That's a matter of perspective," they whispered.

"From ours?"

"No."

"I seek the dead gods," she said.

"There," the old one pointed. "Below."

"Under the mountains?"

"Not mountains."

"What?"

"Gravestones."

"Was that it?" she said.

"What more did you want?" said the
Grim Reaper.

"Just one more day?"

"Ah, but that's what I gave you yesterday."

In a small forgotten casino, the hopeless gambled their memories.

Some played to win a happier past.

The rest were content just to lose.

Zombies splintered the door as she put the gun to her head.

"There's still hope," I lied.

"Not for you," she said, "I only have one bullet."

"What's that knob do?"

"Well, when I turn it this way everything seems OK."

"What if you turn it the other way?"

"Why would I do that?"

Who built the machines?

No one remembers.

What do they do?

Nobody knows.

Protect our homes?

No one remembers.

Keep us hostage?

Nobody knows.

"Well you know, whenever one door closes, another opens," he said.

"Does it? What a strange house you have."

"We think it may be haunted."

"Ghosts see you when you are alone, honest, unguarded," she said.

"They see the real you. If you see a ghost, don't be afraid. Be ashamed."

"You're my best friend, eh boy?" the man said.

The dog wagged his tail.

"And I'm your best friend."

The dog looked away.

It got awkward.

"Would you stop following me around?"

"No can do, I'm haunting you."

"You aren't a ghost."

"Well, not yet, for now I'm just interning."

The ghost of a smile drifted across her lips.

"This is more serious than we thought," said the exorcist.

"Hello," she said, and smiled.

Alarms wailed. Security swarmed in, but it was too late for them to stop.

The smile was already spreading.

"What's wrong?"

"You wouldn't understand."

"Try me."

"Fine," she said, and unfurled six wings. His face melted. She sang the end of time.

The Torturers Guild liked to say that there was no 'i' in 'team.'

And no 'i' in 'torturer.'

And no eyes in anyone, if they had their way.

"Dad, why do Santa's deer have bells?"

"Remember how we put the bell on the cat because he kept eating birds?"

"Yeah?"

"That. But kids."

"I was told snips, snails and puppy-dog tails," Doctor White said, and set down his scalpel.

"But that's not what this looks like at all."

"I'm so tired," she said, "of everyone saying I'm crazy."

"You're talking to me, aren't you?"

"So?"

"Well, for starters, I'm a mailbox."

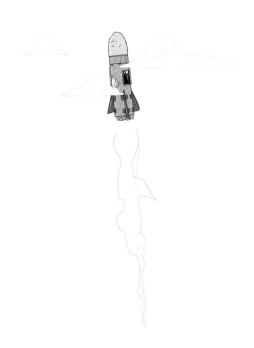

She built herself a rocket ship,

and blasted into space

to see how many years it took

to miss the human race.

"Shoot him! I'm the real Sam," Sam said.

"No, I'm Sam, shoot him," said the other Sam.

"Hi, I'm Tony," said Tony.

"Tony, not now," said Sam.

She

knew that if she nailed her metre,

rhythm clean and rhymes all neat, her

words presented with a twist then

someone might finally listen.

"I caught a ghost!"

"Did you? Where is it?"

"Wherever I go, of course."

"So, it's not caught, you're haunted."

"She said you'd say that."

I built a robot to replace you, but it was short a
crucial part.

So I bought scalpels and some chloroform,
and went hunting for a heart.

He burned the works of greater writers and mixed the ashes into his ink.

But ash isn't fire. The words he wrote still lay cold on the page.

Was she worthless? she wondered.

It felt like it. She'd been so easily set aside.

But every treasure map leads to something left behind.

When the ships appeared we thought they wanted war, to conquer Earth and take all we'd built.

It was worse.

They ignored us, and moved on.

The ship's engines ran on secrets.

To reach the stars, the pilot told it all that she had.

The secrets she saw out there brought her home.

One day, all the magic came back.

Dragons nested on skyscrapers, preening
over reflections.

The fairy folk, forests lost, found Hollywood.

Inspiration was a non-renewable resource, we discovered.

We tried to think of a way to conserve what was left, but we were out of ideas.

"I read your story."

"And?"

"It's so short. Why did it take so long to write?"

"It took time to get all the extra words out of the way."

"This is a magic typewriter," he said.

"Is it?"

"Yeah, anything you type on it comes true."

"Let me try," she said, and typed:

The End

Supporters

Unbound is a new kind of publishing house. Our books are funded directly by readers. This was a very popular idea during the late eighteenth and early nineteenth centuries. Now we have revived it for the internet age. It allows authors to write the books they really want to write and readers to support the books they would most like to see published.

The names listed below are of readers who have pledged their support and made this book happen. If you'd like to join them, visit

www.unbound.com.

Jérôme Abdou
Elbi Adajew
Adam Adam
Scott Adams
Laura Adventourist
Sameer Ajmani
Sean Akers
Brenda Albertz
Amanda Amalfi
Ibrahim S. Amin
Ismail Amin
Khadijah Amin
Tahara Amin
Karen Amoudry
Refik Anadol
Judith Anderson
Melissa Anderson
Deanna Andresen
Ben Armstrong
Claire Armstrong-
  Brealey
Steven Arnott
Jason Arthur
David Astika
Guillaume Athenour
Emma Atkinson

Leeann Atkinson
Jacob Austin
Geoffrey Bachelet
Tamir Bahar
Adam Bailey
Eric Bailey
Richard Bairwell
Katie Baker
Taylor Balbi
Ronnie Ball
Jason Ballinger
Frederikke Bang
Alexandra Bannerman
Marko Banušić
Erinn Barker
Donna Barnes
Ella Barrett
Aaron Bastin-Millar
Hayley Bates
Adrian Bauer
James Beauchamp
Tony Belfer
Ruth Bender
Mathew Benson
Evan Bentley
Kris Bentley

Julian Benton
Shafea Bhaisaheb
Michael Bikovitsky
Daniel Bingham
Emily Birch
Sam Blanchard
Monique Blason
Devin Blatchford
Clare Blick
Roger Blunden
Cole Bogue
Jeffrey Bohr
Michael Bostock
Debra Bourdouklis
Jules Bowes
Michelle Braatz
Kirstin Bradshaw
Leo Breebaart
Petra Breunig
Adam Brewer
Aske Brock
Samuel Brockelbank
Judith Brouwer
Jeremy Brown
Leonie Brown
Ruth Brown

Trevor Brownd
Julian Brownlow
Elly Maria Brus
Samantha Bumgarner
Joseph Burchett
Kate Burgener
Mike Burgess
Carl Burkitt
Ali Burns
Mel Burns
Marcus Butcher
Nico Caballero
Caesuras
Emily Campbell
Rob Cantando
Brody Cardoza
Darren Cardoza
Denise Cardoza
Diana Cardoza
Dustin Cardoza
Dylan Cardoza
Emma Cardoza
D E Carr
Ann Carrier
Joshua Carroll
Mary-Rose Carroll
Angharad Cartwright
Tiago Carvalho
Joseph Cellucci
Stephanie Champion
Liesl Chaplin
Paul Chaplin
Christine Cheverall
Guillaume Chicoisne
Benjamin Chojnacki
Tzevai Chong
Janel Christensen
Quentin Christensen
Charles Chuck
CKetti
Kevin Clack
Larry Clapp
Em Clark
Cara Clarke

Lauren Cleary
Charlie Close
Garrett Coakley
Susan Coleman
Craig Collins
Philip Collins
Kevin Conyers
Adam Cornelius
Sarah Cornell
Gabi Costas
Bryan Cothorn
Janelle Cottrell
Sam Courtney
Zach Cox
Benjamin Coyle
H Crampton
John Crawford
Kim Crawford
Hayley Cruz
Linda Cummings
Thomas Dahms
Alex Darbyshire
Toby Darling
Matthew Darlison
Elizabeth Darracott
Frank David
Matthew Davidson
Travis Davidson
Chloe Davies
Stephanie Davies
Eric Davis
Carol Day
G'pa Day
Tom de Bruin
Pieter De Praetere
Bernard DeCrane
Christopher Deng
Miles Deponty
Laure Deprez
Fernando Diaz
Serge Don
Catherine Donald
Brian Donovan
April Douglas

Kim Dowd
Markie Downing
James Dressel
Ryan Drover
John Drueckhammer
Ada Dubrawska
Dr Andy Dufresne
Millionaire Esquire
Declan Dyer
Maria Easton
Mel Eatherington
Cynthia Eck
Joseph Edwards
Mikael Eiman
Loretta Ekoniak
Saoirse Ellis
Tamar Elmensdorp-
 Lijzenga
Jo Eltzeroth
Matthew Entecott
Brian Ericson
Eric Ericson
Eduardo Espada
Nicolas Estezet
Dylan Evans
Juliet Evans
Lloyd Evans
Kristin Evenson Hirst
Feuf F
Colleen Fagan
Samma Fagan
Roozbeh Farahbod
Amy Farmer
Mandy Farrar
Kamrhan Farwell
Rusty Feeney
Victor Felder
Christine Fenech
Christina Fetzek
Adam Fischlin
Ofir Fishkin
Jamie Flateb
Alison Flynn
Geert Folkertsma

John Forbes
Ed Fox
Emily Fox
Lucent Fox
Joanna Franks
Christina Fraser
Renato Frasson
Jennifer Frick
Michael Fromberger
Sara G
Meredith Gabbott
Stefan Gagne
Mallory Galatzer-Levy
Nigel Galbraith
Hans Gallas
Lilia Gallegos
Chris Garland
Annette Gear
John Geier
Theodoros Georgiou
Revelle Gerson
Adrian Gibbs
Maggie Gilbert
Sara Gille
Ellie Gilroy
Jim Gilsinan
Lena Gkika
Paul Godfrey
Anna Goldberg
Mark Goldfarb
Daniel Gonçalves
Charles Gondre
Ludovica Gonella
George Goodfellow
Marco Götze
Scarlet Gradwell
Ingrid Graudins
Autumn Gravett-Arnold
Matt Gray
Nathan Gray
Brianne Green
Steve Greene
Nathan Grice
Shannon Griffiths

Jessica Grimm
Adam Gross
Natasha Grujic
Alex Gyoshev
Ava H.L.
Jennifer Haig
Cris Hale
Jenna Margaret Hall
Gretel Hallett
Veit Hammerstingl
Kevin Hancock
Edward Hanscom
Jeremy Hanson
Josh Hanson
Penni Hanson
Michael Haren
Karen Harp
Rae Harris
Róisín Harty
Kasra Hashemi
Raisa Hassan
Tara Hatchett
Elizabeth Hauner
Rebecca Haymore
Anssi Matti Helin
Ian Hellström
Kelly Henley
Loretta Henslick
Dan Hermann
Aiko Herrmann
Margaret Herrmann
David Heyman
Alesia Higdon
Amy Higgins
Ciara Higgins
Ahed Hijjawi
Tyler Hill
Samantha Hines
Derek Hironaka
Matt Hodges
Tanner Hodges
Bryan Hoffer
Ellis Hoffman
Anne Hoganson

John Hollowell
Georgiana Holton
Hoon Hong
Mark Hood
Jenni Hopper
Tori Horton
Daphne Howell
Antonia Hoyle
Andrea Huber
Alice Hughes
Ben Hurst
Jessica Hurtgen
Steve Hurwitz
John Iadanza
Gigi Inara
Joshua Inman
Peggy Jackson Irvin
Conrad Irwin
Baylie Isaacs
Jan Ivanov
Biliby Iwai
Jukka Jaatinen
Robert Jacob
Arne Jacobs
Shaun Jafarian
Emma Jarvis
Laura Jellicoe
Jóhannes Birgir Jensson
Karen Jones
Lauren Jones
Matthew Juffs
Lee-Sien Kao
Kate Karn
Magnus Kartvedt
John Katzman
Joshua Keay
Christopher Kellogg
Jessica Kellogg
Steve Kelsey
Jason Kesler
Michelle Khuu
Dan Kieran
Maddy King
Samantha Kingsbury

Andrew Kirby
Jens & Wencke Kirschner
Edo Kleinman
Kate Kligman
Damian Kluba
Ken Kobayashi
Susanne Koch
Peter Kohaut
Thomas Kohl
Doug Kolbicz
Peter Komar
Marek Koniuszewski
John Koutrouba
Achilleas Koutsou
Kip Kozlowski
Christopher Kranz
Aleksander Kraśnicki
Jennifer Kroon
Dom, Sam & Ariadne Kua
Pat Kubik
Andrew Kuo
Daniel Kuzlik
Emma L
Pierre L'Allier
Rachel Lammer
Kevin Lamoree
Devin Lamothe
David Langendries
Ryan Langford
Corey Latislaw
Tom Lavery
Hailey Le
Benjamin Le Guenic
Andrew LeCain
Clinton Lee
Mark Lee
Randy Lee
Antonis Legakis
Adeline Legat
Michael Leinartas
Daniel Lemke
Isabelle Leone

Bethany Leslie
Lies Lesy
Jonathan Li
Judith Licciardello
Chris Lienemann
Ben Liff
Susan Lindsey
Byron Liu
Sebastian Lobato Genco
Léna Lockhart
John Lombardo
Erik Long
Brittany Lopez
Scott Lopez
Iain Lorriman
Arthur Losquiavo
Max Loutzenheiser
Brian Lovelace
Peg Lovelace
Joshua Lowles
Jo Macdonald
Megan MacDonald
José Machado
David & Alexandra Mackintosh
Karen Macleod
Marius Mählen
Eli Mahler
Miska Mäkinen
Joe Maliksi
Travis Malkovich
Azraee Mamat
Sarah Manriquez
Kate Mansfield
David Marchisotto
Karanasou Maria
Eugenio Marletti
Sara Marquette
Frances Marshall
Dan Martin
Danni Martin
Kain Martin
Tyler Martin

David Martins de Matos
Alison Mastny
Marian Matej
Crystal Mathews
Andreas Mathieu
Jim Mathison
David Matkins
Lydia Maxim
Landon Maxwell
Paul May
Frances McCarthy
Quin McCarthy
Taylor McClanahan
Jason McCoy
Jimmy McDermott
Noah McDonald
Wendy McGill
Kevin McGrath
Travis McGruder
Deanna McKenzie
Daniel McLaren
Luke McNamara
Zeus Mendoza
Kat Metcalf
Jesse Meyers
Trisha Michaelson
Melissa Midyett
Eve Milan
Alex Miles
Julio Miles
James Miller
Jefferson Miller
Kevin Miller
Luke Miller
Mark Miller
Mark & Wendy Miller
Nicola Miller
Paul Miller
Rebecca Miller
RJ Miller
Mailea Miller-Pierce
John Mitchinson
Alex Mook
Emily Moore

Carla Morales
Chris Moreno
Skyler Morris
Adam Moszt
Yvonne Moulds
Matt Mullen
Andrew Murdoch
Emmalene Murphy
Mikhail Musienko
Justin Myers
Carlo Navato
Carlos Negrete
Melissa Nelson
Nick Newman
Kristin Nielsen
Alexander Nirenberg
Jeff Nivin
Parker Nokes
Robert Nordendahl
Catherine Norman
Tom Nugent
James O'Connor
Marc Obaldo
Jared Oberkirsch
Georgia Odd
Jamie Ogle
Angela Ohland
Lyndsey Ohland
Dag Øien
Matthew Olander
G Oommen
Judith Orr
Jim Ortiz
Oscar
Espen Sae-Tang
Ottersen
Erin Ottley
Justin Otto
Thomas Owen
Candice Ozorowicz
Emily Ozsvald
Heather Padgett
Stephanie Pagani
Michael Panuschka

Glenn Pareira
Isaac Parker
Jon Pavelich
Paweł Pawlik
Hendrik Payer
Susan Peinsipp
Joseph Penney
Veeva Penney
Robert Perce
Felicia Perkins
Hugo Perks
Simon Persoff
Jonathan Persson
Sarah Pettis
Magnus Peveri
Amanda Phillips
Bryanna Phillips
Jeremy Phillips
Raúl Pineda
Niki Pladson
Michele Playfair
Sebastiano Poggi
David Polk
Justin Pollard
Michael Popeney
Alfred Portengen
Gregg Porter
Ashley Powell
Janet Pretty
Rhian Price
Nathan Primeau
Joshua Pruett
Avi Pryntz-Nadworny
Jeff Pulice
Sean Rafferty
Gavin Ralph
Michael Rasmussen
Aleksandra Ravas
Shane Ravenn
BD Ravi
Simon Reap
Lisa Redden
Kate Reed
M.E. Reese

Helen Reid
Craig Reilly
Adam Renberg Tamm
Phyllis Richardson
Simon Richter
Svante Richter
Nadia Rickards
Julie Rickerson
Joost Rijneveld
Julia Vanessa Rilling
Craig Ritchie
Brian Roath
Edward Robbins
Brian Roberts
Nichole Robertson
Sebastian Rocca
Kelly Roche
Alexandre Rochon
Frank Rodolf
Josh Rontal
Matt Roper
Vashti Ross
Luca Rossetto
Debi Roth Sparks
Jordi Rovira i Bonet
Leo Rubinkowski
Cosima Rughinis
Klaas Jan Runia
Jacob Ryde
Jason Salaz
Jeremy Sale
Arttu Salonen
Stephen Sandsmith
Ezequiel Sapoznicoff
Brendan Sargeant
Siddhartha Sarkar
Lionel Sausin
Tracy Sayo
Michelle Scaccianoce
Brandon Scheel
Andy Scheffler
Josh Scheibe
Justus Schmidt
Rick Schulte

Ariann Schultz
Jeff Scott
Justine Scott
Reuben Scott
Alan Sears
John Seiffer
Sarit Semo
Allan Setash
Andrei Sevcenco
Adam Shaffer
Alekhya Shastri
Fraser Shaw
Donna Sheeders
Jenny Sheridan
Mark Shields
Pavel Sikora
Theresa Simard
Miriam Sincell Burton
Rishi Sinha
Evan Sitt
Debra Skeer
Jonny Skyboss
Sam Slessor
Jasmynne Sloan
Alice Smith
Carolyn Smith
Matthew Smith
Patrick Smith
Zane Smith
Sherri & Will Snow
Anne Sowell
Nicole Sparks
Henriette B. Stavis
Mark Steenbakkers
Dirk Steindorf
Kristen Stewart
Zorica Stojchevska
Eleanor Stone
Shel Strickland
Samantha Sturm
Niko Suave
Joel Suplido
Bobby Tables
Remo Tamayo

Kathleen Tappin
David Tarr
Jane Taylor
Linden Taylor
Marc Taylor
TJ Taylor
Techxplorer
Evan Terrell
Monica Terry
Ralf Teusner
Eileen The
Benjamin Thomas
Elaine Thomas
Sheila Thomas
Joanna Thompson
Liza Thompson
Mike Thompson
Alexa Thorne
Christopolis Tiberius
Drew Timms
James Tomkins
Christian Tomlins
Diego Torres
Kathleen Trembath
Anke Tröder
Bing Turkby
Natalia Ujlaki
Ferdinand Uy
Rens van Bergeijk
Gert Van Gool
Sam Van Zeebroeck
Bethany Venn
Romain Vernisse
Gale Vester
Micki Vildershøj
Amrei Voigt
Wouter Vos
Viola Voß
Aaron Wadler
Mark Wales
James Walker
Sam Walker
Steve Walker
Nick Walpole

G Ward
Matthew Warhol
John Warner
Wendy Warren
Rhiannon Warwick
William Weber Silva
Eliza Weetch
Chris Weigert
Alan Wendt
Tamie Wiggins
Jascha Wilken
Ann Williams
Dave Williams
Garry Williams
Michael & Kathy
Williams
Rob Winkler
Anthony Winter
Laura Winter
Robert Winterhalter
Marco Winther
Don Wise
Adam Witte
Lina Witzner
Michael Wojcikiewicz
R. Wolf
Sheryl Wolfe
Adrian Woodfield
Annabelle Woodger
Katherine Woolfitt
Nick Wray
Shafik Yaghmour
Olga Yatsenko
J. D. Nick Yinger
Peter Young
Reuben Youngblom
Sahoko Yui
David Zabner
Edgars Zaķis
Johan Zandin
Michael Ziörjen
Nicole Zonnenberg
Matthijs Zwinderman